THE ART OF THE
REAL
USA 1948-1968

E. C. GOOSSEN

THE ART OF THE
REAL

USA 1948-1968

THE MUSEUM OF MODERN ART, NEW YORK

DISTRIBUTED BY NEW YORK GRAPHIC SOCIETY LTD., GREENWICH, CONNECTICUT

© The Museum of Modern Art, 1968
11 West 53 Street, New York, New York 10019
Library of Congress Catalogue Card Number 68-29837
Designed by Joseph B. Del Valle
Cover designed by Donald E. Munson
Printed in the U.S.A. by Eastern Press, Inc.

Preface and Acknowledgments

This book, as well as the exhibition it was designed to accompany, is based on the premise that a significant, identifiable change has been taking place in American art over the last two decades. The diversity of the styles that have appeared may at first seem simply confusing, ranging as they do from pop art's immersion in subject matter to op art's appeal to pure visual sensation. Yet between these extremes there can be seen a consistent development of abstract forms and the manner of their presentation. We have witnessed, for example, an interaction, perhaps unprecedented in modern art, between painting and sculpture. In this development seems to lie the essence of the most crucial problem for art in our time, and also the most significant area of stylistic invention.

Every style of the period, of course, is relevant in its way to this fundamental change. It would have been possible to include here examples of pop art, but they would have been visually distracting in this context; op art has also made a major contribution, especially in the realm of ideas about perception, but it too would have introduced unnecessary complications. It was further felt that the juxtaposition of works of art largely similar in formal means would allow their distinct differences to emerge. Thus the seeming narrowness of the selection is hopefully to be understood as a matter of purpose rather than of prejudice.

The generosity of artists and collectors and galleries who lent works to the exhibition, knowing its intent, is therefore especially commendable. Artists have a natural aversion to being categorized or treated didactically—especially when they are in the midstream of their careers. No disrespect, however, has been intended toward individual works. The quality of each was the deciding factor in its inclusion. It is to be hoped that those disagreeing with the thesis will nevertheless have the opportunity to enjoy the works, each on its own premises.

Some of the works chosen are familiar, but were included because of their historical significance; most of them, however, have seldom or never been seen before, and several were made specifically for this occasion. Thanks should go to all those individuals and galleries who lent works to the exhibition, with special thanks to the artists themselves, who made available more than half the works shown. The director, who presented this exhibition by invitation, also wishes to extend his thanks to the members of the Museum staff who gave him untiring assistance: René d'Harnoncourt, Director, who gave support to the idea of the show from its inception; Waldo Rasmussen, Director of Circulating Exhibitions, whose interest and cooperation have been inspiring throughout the preparation of the exhibition; Alicia Legg, Associate Curator of Painting and Sculpture, who helped in all aspects of it; Wilder Green, Director of the Exhibitions Program, the architect of the installation, whose sensitivity to the problem and to the works is reflected in its ultimate achievement; Dorothy Miller, Senior Curator of Painting and Sculpture, who made possible the several loans from the Museum collection; and Jane Necol, whose assistance far exceeded that of mere secretarial efficiency.

E. C. Goossen
Director of the Exhibition

To propose that some art is more "real" than other art may be foolhardy. Yet many American artists over the last few years have made this proposal by the nature of their works. They have taken a stance that leaves little doubt about their desire to confront the experiences and objects we encounter every day with an exact equivalence in art. That they are shaping this equivalence by modifying forms inherited from the history of modern abstraction may or may not be an accident. Certainly there seems to be a growing distrust of idealism and its unfulfilled promises. The "real" of today as it is posited by this new art has nothing to do with metaphor, or symbolism, or any kind of metaphysics. It is not the ideal Hegelian essence that Hans Hofmann was invoking several decades ago in his essay, "The Search for the *Real.*"[1] It does not wish to convey the notion that reality is somewhere else. Neither is it related to the *symbolic* reality Malevich thought he had discovered when, in 1913, he first isolated his black square on a white field. Malevich indeed had produced a *real* square, but he employed it as an element in the construction of a precariously balanced, idealized order with which he proposed to bring forth a "new world of feeling." Today's "real," on the contrary, makes no direct appeal to the emotions, nor is it involved in uplift. Indeed, it seems to have no desire at all to justify itself, but instead offers itself for whatever its uniqueness is worth—in the form of the simple, irreducible, irrefutable object.

Whatever the urgencies of the last decade outside the arts that may have helped bring about this insistence on the stubbornly literal idea of the "real," there is sufficient evidence to explain it purely as an extension of the implications, of both form and attitude, in abstract expressionism.

Of late, as "formalist" criticism bears down harder (out of necessity, one might add), the ambition and the attitude that gave rise to the works of the abstract expressionists have begun to recede behind tomes of analysis. Yet the impetus toward the mature styles of Pollock, Rothko, Still, and Newman (pp. 14-17), to name the four whose influence has persisted most strongly, was the desire to find one's real self on the canvas through personal imagery and format. This desire was not mystical or metaphysical; quite the opposite. It was an overriding ambition to make something so original that its reality could not be challenged. As Clyfford Still wrote in 1952, "We are now committed to an unqualified act, not illustrating outworn myths or contemporary alibis. One must accept total responsibility for what he executes."[2]

1. Hans Hofmann, *Search for the Real and Other Essays* ed. Sara T. Weeks and Bartlett H. Hayes, Jr. (Andover, Mass.: Addison Gallery of American Art, 1948), pp. 46-54; revised ed. (Cambridge, Mass.: The M.I.T. Press, 1967), pp. 40-48.
2. From a letter dated February 5, 1952; quoted in *15 Americans* (New York: The Museum of Modern Art, 1952), p. 22, and *The New American Painting* (New York: The Museum of Modern Art, 1959), p. 76.

These painters had of course learned much from the abstract art of the preceding four decades. They knew that to specify an illusionistic space on an otherwise obviously flat surface inevitably carries representational associations with it. Representation is in turn associated with real*ism,* an illusion of the fact rather than the fact itself. Thus they worked to achieve a feeling of indeterminable space without specifying its dimensions. Imagery had also to be as free from associations as possible and refer to nothing outside its role in the picture. They turned their backs on Euclidean geometry, with its familiar, idealist history, and also gradually removed any overt reference to organic form. Color had to share the burden of originality, as each artist sought to make it as much his own as possible, not only by his selection of hues and values, but also by a personalized method of application that would distinguish it materially from conventional practice. And while they spoke much of subject matter, their aim was not to *represent* something, but to *make* something, something which had never existed in the world before. They wanted, as Mark Rothko said, to eliminate "all obstacles between the painter and the idea, and between the idea and the observer." Among the obstacles he included "memory, history, or geometry."[3]

The forms and formats these artists employed now seem comparatively rich and complex when one becomes used to the minimal paintings of the 1960's. But the high intensity they were able to evoke, using nothing but abstract forms on a two-dimensional surface, set a tone and level that would rarely be matched in the subsequent twenty years, and strangely enough only by those who dared reduce the means even further, while at the same time seeking an even more literal reality.

The early 1950's saw the full efflorescence of abstract expressionism in the hands of its inventors, and also its degradation in the hands of those artists who followed the superficial aspects of "action" painting and depended upon personality alone to carry the day. Such an individualistic approach was not for everybody. Happily there was an alternative. It came from artists of a different temperament, those who felt more at home with the clean, bright, unmodulated colors of De Stijl, the sharp-edged forms of the American precisionists, and the anonymous paint surfaces of the "magic realists." Painting for artists of this persuasion became a process of thought from the very beginning, rather than a process of discovery after the fact, as was the habit of "painterly" expressionists. The objection that such an approach was closer to "design" than to "art" was based on the same romantic prejudice that Jane Austen had tried to correct in *Sense and Sensibility:* i.e., that intellection obviates feeling.

3. From a statement in *The Tiger's Eye* (New York), October 1949; quoted in *15 Americans,* p. 18, and *The New American Painting,* p. 68.

It is a fact, however, that a number of artists with design or architectural training were to take up painting during the 1950's and help to bring about a healthy reaction to expressionistic excess. At first they were relatively obscure; for example, Alexander Liberman was the only painter of the new "hard-edge" school to be included in the important exhibition *Younger American Artists* organized by James Johnson Sweeney in 1954 at the Guggenheim Museum. Liberman's painting had been done in 1950, the same year as *Minimum* (p. 22). At the same time Tony Smith was developing a modular system for his painting (p. 19), and Ellsworth Kelly was in Europe establishing his own stylistic direction. In 1954 Kelly returned from Paris, where he had met Vantongerloo and Jean Arp; neither of these men, however, had much influence on him. Except for a few paintings based on Arp's theories of "chance," most of Kelly's work, then as now, derived from direct observation of forms in his environment. This fascination with things seen, and the way they actually *are* seen, is reminiscent of the prophetic work of Georgia O'Keeffe. In its uncompromising objectivity, O'Keeffe's intense vision seems more coordinate with the art of the last decade than with that of her own generation. A comparison of her *Lake George Window* of 1929 (p. 12) with Kelly's reconstruction of a window observed (p. 13) points up not only our sense of what is factually real in each, but also how the real can be achieved in either two or three dimensions. Certain components of the situation can be equated: the angle of vision is head on, axial symmetry is frankly accepted, composition literally follows fact, and there is no implication of action that would require our suspension of disbelief. O'Keeffe's window is not sculptural beyond the minimal shadowing of delineation, and Kelly's window is not pictorial beyond the illusions inherent in our own seeing. Both are almost totally static and make no allusions to any world other than their own, yet they are "art" as much as are any other works of art.

During this same period Kelly discovered the power of pure color. He painted a series of pictures made up of joined, vertical panels. Each panel was painted one unmodulated color emphasizing its rectangular area and its relative physical position in a horizontal format similar to an ordinary color chart. In such pictures as *Painting for a White Wall,* 1952 (p. 25), Kelly literally turned color into subject matter. A few years later other artists would employ this format for the same reason, but none of them would surpass the purity, innocence, and sensuous presence of color that Kelly achieved in these paintings. He was also responsible for what was probably the first "shaped canvas" that can be directly related to subsequent developments. *White Relief* of 1952-1955 (p. 23) did not issue from a drawing board but from the observation of the mirror-image of light streaming under the arch of a bridge. Although it is not necessary to know Kelly's sources to experience his art as art, knowing them helps one understand why his work has such structural integrity.

Even among artists who stayed with representational, rather than abstract, subject matter, common sense and literalness have played major roles. Jasper Johns possesses both to a maximum degree. To solve the problem of subject matter in relation to the flat canvas, and perhaps taking a hint from O'Keeffe's leaf pictures of the 1920's, he often selected flat subjects like targets, maps, typographical elements, or flags. Others, committed to solving the problem in terms of an abstraction without allusion, took longer and more difficult routes. Both the younger Frank Stella and the older Paul Feeley had, by the late 1950's, found themselves frustrated trying to climb the ramparts of abstract expressionism. Each began to look for a rational way to redirect his art. Stella abandoned variegated color and painterliness; starting with a rectangle or cross, like many city planners, he enlarged upon it by a simple series of equally broad stripes until a satisfactory area for the module of the stripe was reached, and that was his picture (p. 28). The external shape was determined by the initial shape at the center, and in order not to end up with leftover areas at the edges, which would have created the image of a heraldic device on a field, he notched them out. The result was a "shaped canvas." In later experiments (p. 29) with V's, parallelograms, rhomboids, hexagons, semi-circles, etc., he invented series after series of interpenetrating and overlaid shapes using color coding, as Stuart Davis had in his late pictures, to identify and hold the colored bands within a minimal, flattened space.

Feeley, on the other hand, seeing the problem as one of keeping alive the surface of the canvas without losing its flatness, developed an interchangeable relationship of figure to ground by means of two undulating, interactive shapes. When one or the other was placed on an unpainted canvas field, the reverberation with the absent but implied figure gave life to the picture as a whole (pp. 31-33). Ultimately he also created these shapes in intersecting planes of painted wood, or in fully round constructions of fiber glass exposing them to three-dimensional space (p. 30).

There were painters, nevertheless, throughout the 1950's and early 1960's who did not seek to relieve the pressure on two-dimensional painting by moving toward or into the third dimension. In fact, they added still more pressure. Turning to their expressionist forebears, they tended to pick a particular element or quality from the work of Rothko or Newman or Still, emphasize it, and then make it carry the main burden of pictorial means and interest. The urge, in other words, was to reduce rather than to agglomerate (the reverse was likely to be true of those who followed the tradition of the "action" painters). This reduction also occurred in the over-all design of their pictures, in the direction either of "field" painting or in the symmetrical organization of centered, simplified non-images.

Following Still's tacky paint surface, for example, Ralph Humphrey eliminated Still's kind of drawing, shape, and suggestion of planes, and ended up with a field of color (p. 51). He modulated his color with very slight shifts of hue and worked the paint into low, light-catching relief, achieving a subtle, tactile physical presence across the canvas. Ad Reinhardt, on the other hand, who had often been considered as one of the abstract expressionists but was never quite able to abandon his Bauhaus prejudices, worked from within nearly opaque colors, often matte black, illuminating an elementary cruciform with lighter tints. The near-objectness of the black pictures in particular was to have considerable impact on some of the younger artists, among them sculptors, of the later 1960's.

A number of painters during the late 1950's and early 1960's contributed to the reduction of imagery and incident without quite abandoning expressionism. Ray Parker, for example (p. 34), seems to have been torn between lyrical passion and the need to find a way to make his art as palpably real as possible. There are lyrical qualities, too, in Morris Louis' work, but they are balanced by the physicality of the soak-stain method he used, which identifies color with the actual weave of the canvas. Moreover, Louis kept reducing his means, and even the area that the hues occupied in the vast expanse of raw canvas, ever seeking a still higher brilliance to confirm their existence as color. And in the last series before his death, referred to as the "Unfurleds" (p. 38), he pushed the central space between the ribbons of color more widely apart, thereby increasing the distance over which the eye must travel to pull the image together, or, if one's gaze is fixed on the empty center, calling peripheral vision into action. These two ways of seeing such pictures adds to our perception of their physical existence as space-occupying objects.

Kenneth Noland's most recent pictures are even larger than Louis', and something similar occurs in respect to peripheral vision. But since Noland carries his variegated horizontal stripes across the whole field, the eye can only handle parts at a time, except when the picture is seen from one end, where the perspective effect of dimunition assists one's understanding of the physical situation. The speed of recognition is slowed, however, by the number of the vertically stacked colors. This stacking, of course, is a system of ordering that has been in wide usage in the sculpture of the 1960's and was employed as early as 1956 by David Smith in the unique piece Five Units Equal (p. 26). It is nonetheless consistent with Noland's earlier concentric circles (p. 39) and his chevron pictures. Noland's ideas for pictorial

format seem to have come from military insignia, selected not for their iconographic implications, but for their banal simplicity, permitting maximum emphasis on color.

The increase in the sheer size of paintings, and recently of sculpture as well, has been a much discussed subject since the days of the big canvases of the abstract expressionists. As painting has become more "minimalist," the optimum sizes appear to have increased proportionately. The same kind of inverse ratio seems to have been at work in another way. As this kind of art has grown more conceptual, it has depended more and more upon such basic responses as simple perception, sensuous appreciation, kinesthetics, and recognition of the tactile, objective existence of the work before us. This may explain the current popularity of sculpture, particularly of abstract and non-pictorial sculpture. Painting, always more capable of, and therefore more prone to, intellectualization, has nevertheless tried to keep pace with this demand for palpable reality, while still remaining painting. It has succeeded so far only by distilling its means and putting more perceptual burdens on the viewer. In a minimal painting by Patricia Johanson (p. 55), for example, we are expected to grasp a single narrow strip of color extending as much as twenty-eight feet along the middle of an empty field of raw canvas. Such pictures remind us that painting had reached the minimal several times before in this century—in O'Keeffe's Blue Lines of 1916 (p. 10), for example, and in Malevich's White on White of 1918—but in the Johanson we are asked to cope with the irreducible facts physically rather than intellectually.

The problem of color in sculpture may never be resolved satisfactorily, since painted sculpture tends to become pictorial, or at least to undergo a serious weakening of form. Color seems to work best with minimalist sculpture, as in some of Lyman Kipp's larger pieces (p. 44) or in Sanford Wurmfeld's three-dimensional color charts (p. 45). As for John McCracken's slabs of sheer color (p. 50), it is hard to tell whether one is confronting a painting or a sculpture.

At this juncture the two modes are still checking out each other's territory to find out what is real for each, suggesting that a more coordinated sense of style may be in the offing. This is especially observable in the common application of simple and regularized patterns and systems: the grid, the modular, and the radial as well as close-packing, stacking, etc. The result is a democratic ordering of similar parts brought together into a totality. Hierarchical passions and dynamics are left behind, and we are faced instead with self-evident, crystalline structure, the objectively (instead of subjectively) real. What is surprising is the variety that such sculpture and painting have been able to provide, given conditions and limitations that we once might have thought

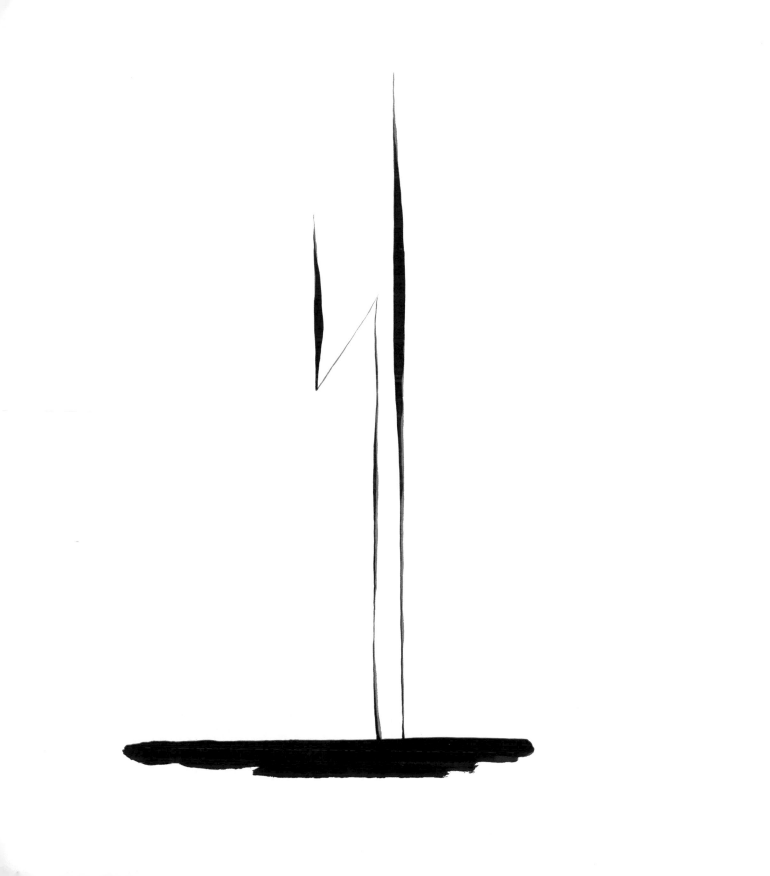

could lead only to empty repetition and boredom.

This variety is partly the result of the interchange between the two modes, which had already begun in the early 1960's. We discover that Carl Andre's earliest stacked sculptures (p. 27) are distinctly related to Stella's first black pictures (p. 28); Darby Bannard's paired rectangles (p. 35) suggest a number of box and plane pieces by Robert Morris (p. 47), Donald Judd, and others; while Agnes Martin's stacked and grid structures (p. 40) find their equivalent in Judd's wall sculptures (pp. 41, 42), Larry Poons's grid paintings, and Sol LeWitt's space cages (p. 43). But when we put all these and other seemingly similar works together, subtle differences appear, and the full richness of the new vocabulary of forms becomes visible.

Whereas Judd and Morris, who have already attracted considerable attention here and abroad, set out to make original and "specific" objects (Judd's term) and have often concerned themselves with the orderly placement of separate units in a space field, Tony Smith has taken an entirely different route. Though he says he "speculates in pure form," the results are hardly speculative. Die and Free Ride (pp. 36-37), both of 1962, are the simplest possible resolutions of the essence of the cube. To confront one of these works is to know the cube on a scale that allows us to experience it fully without being handed ideas about it. The later pieces, following the logic and the variations possible to tetrahedra, can be viewed from any direction whatever without the mass becoming lost in silhouette, a failing of much pictorial sculpture. Smith's attack allows for the broadest range, from pieces that stand aloof and alone to those that can, like Stinger (p. 49), envelop the viewer and force him to experience them. Perhaps more than any other sculptor at this time, Smith has found the precise amount of the "real" we can bear in art, for his work has a monumental power rarely available to other approaches.

The gradual divorce of the physical means of art from expressionistic associations has been accompanied by a distinct change in attitude toward what art should attempt. Expressionism, even at its most abstract, continued many aspects of representational art, and constructivism, despite its purist look, was basically nostalgic in its search for meaning through traditional methods of composition. The new attitude has been turning art inside out: instead of perceptual experience being accepted as the means to an end, it has become the end in itself. The Renaissance artist labored over perspective in order to create an illusion of space within which he could make believable the religious and philosophical ideals of his time; the contemporary artist labors to make art itself believable. Consequently the very means of art have been isolated and exposed, forcing the spectator to perceive himself in the process of his perception. The spectator is not given symbols, but facts, to make of them what he can. They do not direct his mind nor call up trusted cores of experience, but lead him to the point where he must evaluate his own peculiar responses. Thus, what was once concealed within art—the technical devices employed by the artist—is now overtly revealed; and what was once the outside—the meaning of its forms—has been turned inside. The new work of art is very much like a chunk of nature, a rock, a tree, a cloud, and possesses much the same hermetic "otherness." Whether this kind of confrontation with the actual can be sustained, whether it can remain vital and satisfying, it is not yet possible to tell.

E.C.G.

Opposite:
Georgia O'Keeffe. Blue Lines Number 10. 1916. Watercolor on paper, 25 x 19 inches. Lent by Georgia O'Keeffe and The Metropolitan Museum of Art, Alfred Stieglitz Collection, 1949

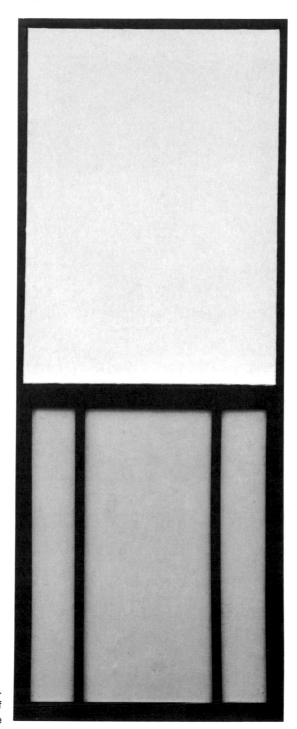

Opposite:

Georgia O'Keeffe. *Lake George Window*. 1929.
Oil on canvas, 40 x 30 inches. The Museum of
Modern Art, New York, acquired through the
Richard D. Brixey Bequest

Above:

Ellsworth Kelly. *Window (Museum of Modern
Art, Paris).* 1949. Oil on canvas, and wood, 50½
x 19½ inches. Owned by the artist

Left:
Mark Rothko. *Number 10.* 1950. Oil on canvas, 90⅜ x 57⅛ inches. The Museum of Modern Art, New York, gift of Philip Johnson

Opposite left:
Barnett Newman. *Day One.* 1951. Oil on canvas, 11 feet x 4 feet 2¼ inches. Whitney Museum of American Art, New York, gift of the Friends of the Whitney Museum and purchase

Opposite right:
Barnett Newman. *Ulysses.* 1952. Oil on canvas, 11 feet x 4 feet 2 inches. Collection Mrs. Barnett Newman, New York

16

Opposite:

Clyfford Still. *Painting.* 1951. Oil on canvas, 7 feet 10 inches x 6 feet 10 inches. The Museum of Modern Art, New York, Blanchette Rockefeller Fund

Above:

Jackson Pollock. *Number 1.* 1948. Oil on canvas, 5 feet 8 inches x 8 feet 8 inches. The Museum of Modern Art, New York, purchase

Left:
Barnett Newman. *Here*. 1950. Bronze, 8 feet x 27 inches x 26 inches. Collection Mrs. Barnett Newman, New York

Opposite:
Tony Smith. *The Louisenberg.* 1953-1954. Oil on canvas, 9 feet 9 inches x 11 feet 7 inches (11 works from a modular series). For owners, see Catalogue 45

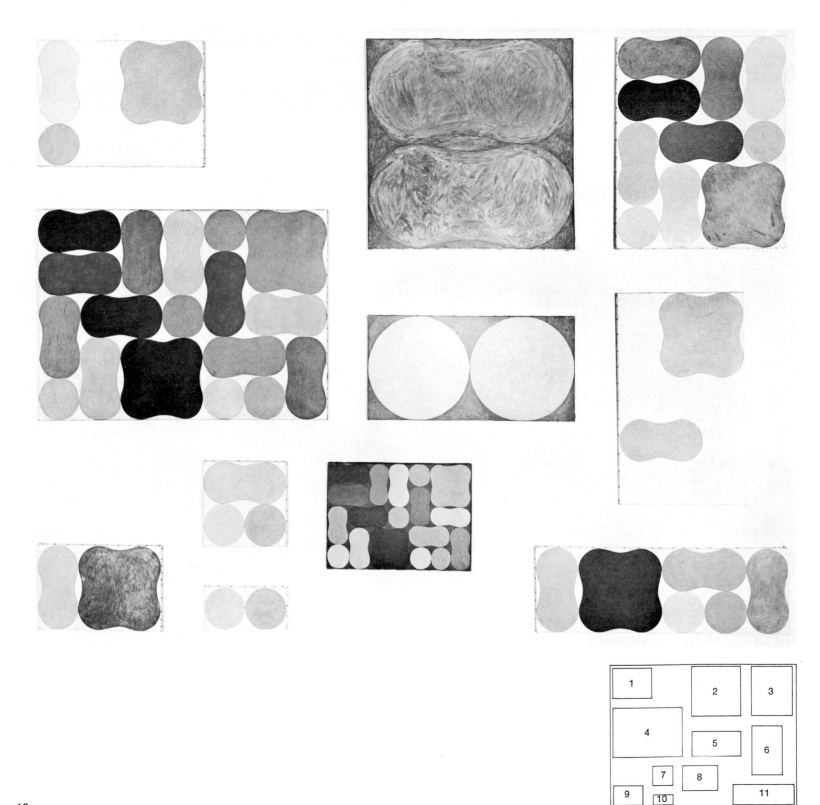

Jasper Johns. *White Numbers.* 1957. Encaustic on canvas, 34 x 28⅛ inches.
The Museum of Modern Art, New York, Elizabeth Bliss Parkinson Fund

Jasper Johns. *Flag.* 1954. Encaustic on newspaper over composition board, 42⅜ x 60¾ inches.
Collection Philip Johnson, New York

Alexander Liberman. *Minimum*. 1950. Enamel on composition board, 48 x 48 inches. Owned by the artist

Ellsworth Kelly. *White Relief—Arch and Its Shadow (Pont de la Tournelle, Paris).* 1952-1955.
Painted wood, 64 x 48 inches. Private collection, London

Opposite:
Ellsworth Kelly. *Colors for a Large Wall.* 1951. Oil on canvas, 64 joined panels, 8 x 8 feet. Sidney Janis Gallery, New York

Above:
Ellsworth Kelly. *Painting for a White Wall.* 1952. Oil on canvas, 5 joined panels, 23½ x 71½ inches. Owned by the artist

Opposite:
David Smith. *Five Units Equal.* 1956. Stainless steel, 74¼ x 16¼ x 14¼ inches. Storm King Art Center, Mountainville, New York

Right:
Carl Andre. *Cedar Piece.* 1960-1964. Cedarwood, 72 x 36¼ x 36¼ inches. Collection Hollis Frampton, New York

 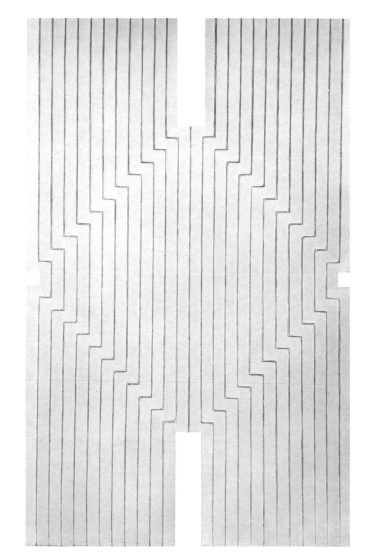

Above left:
Frank Stella. *Turkish Mambo.* 1959-1960. Oil on canvas, 11 feet 6 inches x 7 feet 6¾ inches. Private collection, New York

Above right:
Frank Stella. *Newstead Abbey.* 1960. Metallic paint on canvas, 10 x 6 feet. Private collection, New York. (Not in exhibition)

Opposite:
Frank Stella. *Tuftonboro I.* 1966. Synthetic polymer paint on canvas, 8 feet 3 inches x 9 feet 1 inch. Collection Mr. and Mrs. Victor W. Ganz, New York

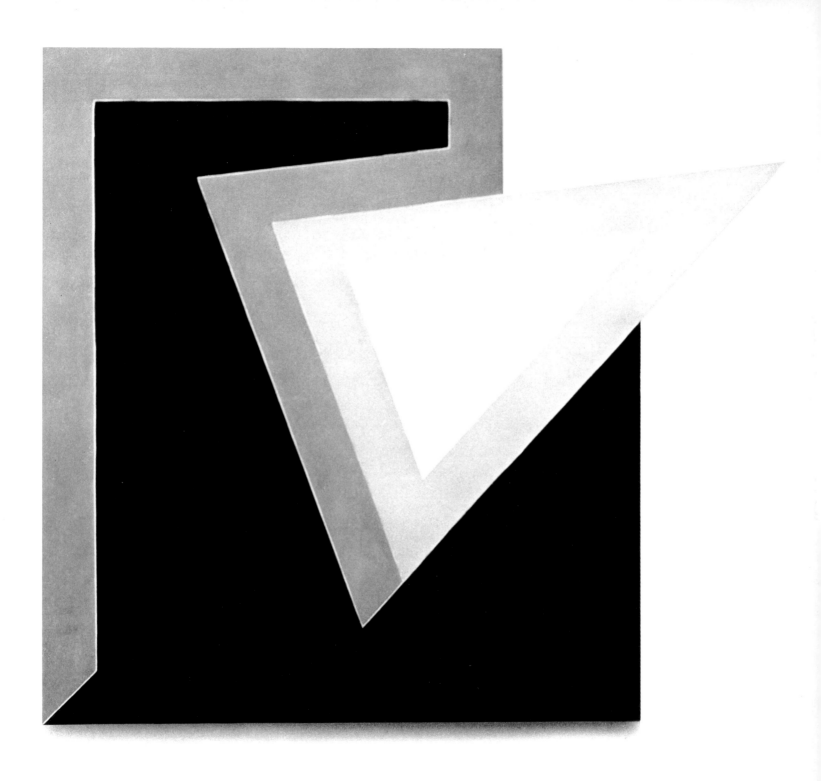

Above left:
Paul Feeley. *Deneb-El-Algedi*. 1965. Painted plywood, 36 x 36 x 36 inches. Estate of the artist, courtesy Betty Parsons Gallery, New York

Above right:
Paul Feeley. Model for *Jack*. 1965. Painted wood, 8 x 8 x 8 inches. Collection Helen Webster Feeley, North Bennington, Vermont

Opposite:
Paul Feeley. *Alphecca*. 1965. Oil on canvas, 60 x 60 inches. Estate of the artist, courtesy Betty Parsons Gallery, New York

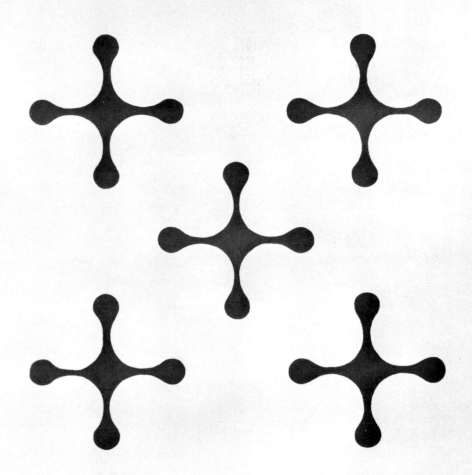

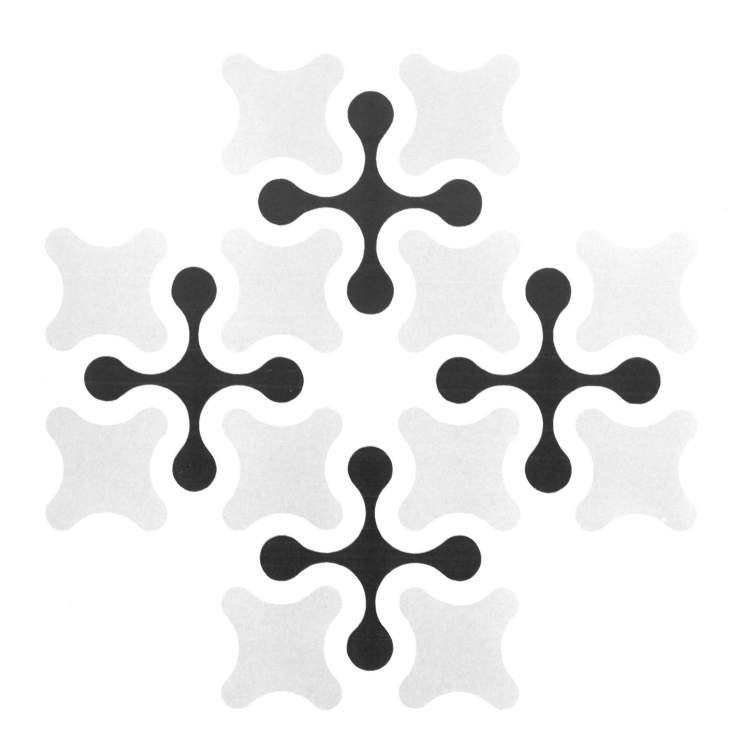

Paul Feeley. *Grafias*. 1965. Enamel on canvas, 92 x 92 inches. Collection Helen Webster Feeley, North Bennington, Vermont

Paul Feeley. *Ilion.* 1962. Oil on canvas, 60 x 48 inches. Estate of the artist, courtesy Betty Parsons Gallery, New York

Opposite:
Raymond Parker. *Number 100.* 1962. Oil on canvas, 77 x 68 inches. Owned by the artist

Below:
Darby Bannard. *Allure-Allure.* 1961. Oil on canvas, 67 x 63 inches. Owned by the artist, lent courtesy Tibor de Nagy Gallery, New York

4488

Above:
Tony Smith. *Die.* 1962. Steel, 6 x 6 x 6 feet. Collection Samuel J. Wagstaff, Jr., Hartford, Connecticut

Opposite:
Tony Smith. *Free Ride.* 1962. Steel, 6 feet 8 inches x 6 feet 8 inches x 6 feet 8 inches. Collection David M. Pincus, Wynnewood, Pennsylvania

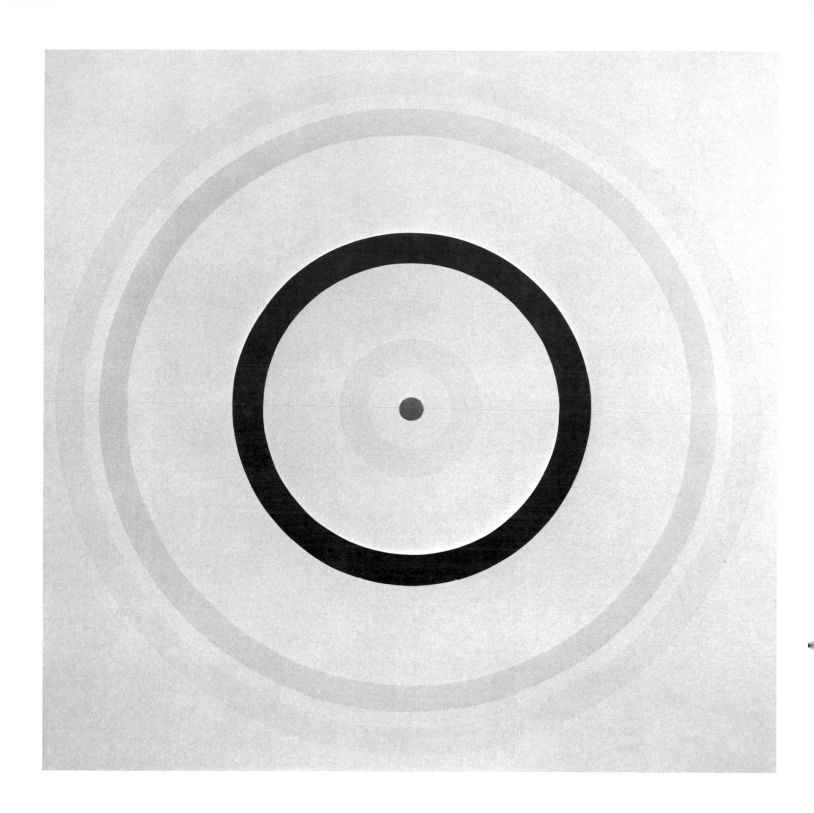

Opposite:
Kenneth Noland. *Turnsole.* 1961. Oil on canvas, 7 feet 10⅛ inches x 7 feet 10⅛ inches. The Museum of Modern Art, New York, Blanchette Rockefeller Fund

Above:
Morris Louis. *Alpha Tau.* 1961. Acrylic on canvas, 8 feet 6 inches x 19 feet 6 inches. City Art Museum of St. Louis, gift of the Shoenberg Foundation

Opposite:
Agnes Martin. *Bones Number 2.* 1961. Oil on canvas, 72 x 48 inches. Collection Betty Parsons, New York

Right:
Donald Judd. Untitled. 1965. Galvanized iron, 11 feet 3 inches high (8 boxes, each 9 x 40 x 31 inches, at 9-inch intervals). Collection Henry Geldzahler, New York

Above:
Donald Judd. Untitled. 1963. Painted wood and galvanized iron, 49⅞ x 42 x 5½ inches. Owned by the artist

Opposite:
Sol LeWitt. Model for untitled sculpture. 1966. Painted wood, 2 x 12 x 12 feet. Dwan Gallery, New York

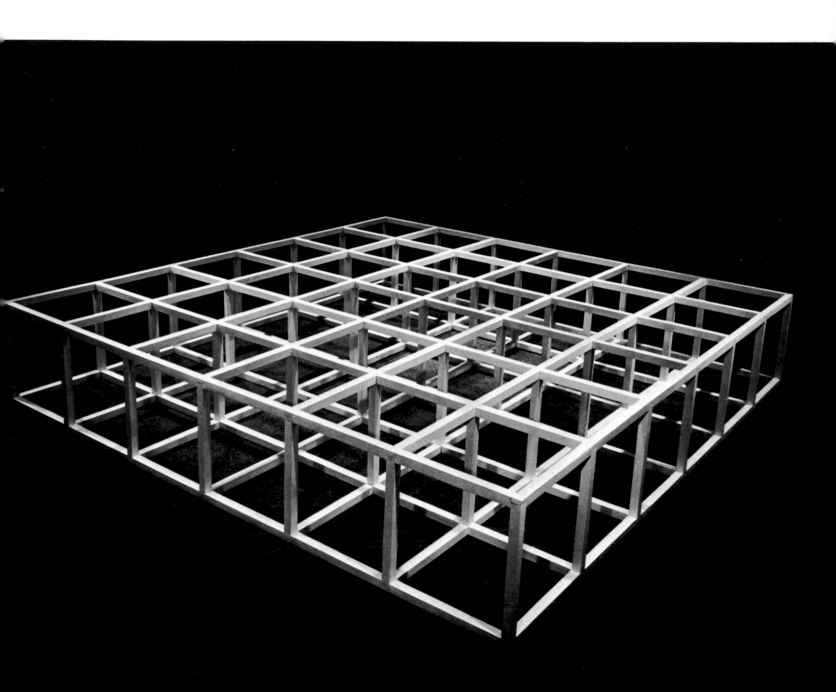

Left:
Lyman Kipp. Model for *Albatross*. 1968. Painted wood, 9 inches high

Opposite:
Sanford Wurmfeld. *III—12*. 1967-1968. Painted wood, 7 feet 6 inches high, diameter 30 inches. Owned by the artist, lent courtesy Tibor de Nagy Gallery, New York

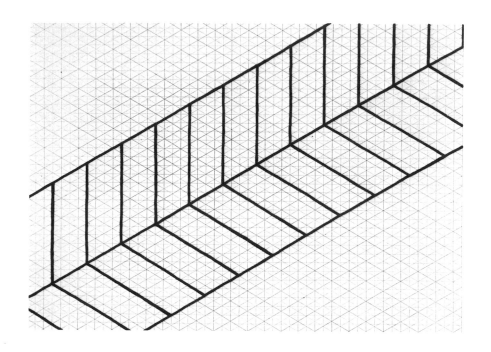

Above:
Carl Andre. Study for *Fall.* 1967. Pen and ink on graph paper

Opposite:
Robert Morris. Untitled. 1967-1968. Aluminum I-beams, 4 feet 6 inches x 15 feet x 15 feet. Leo Castelli Gallery, New York

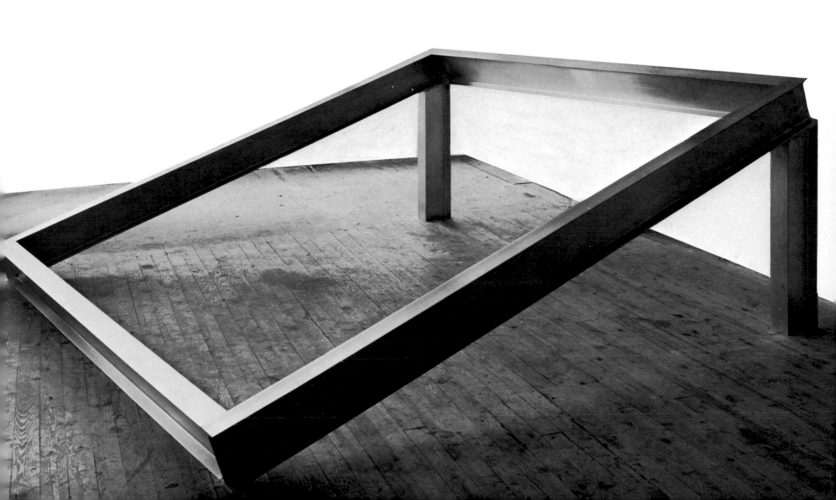

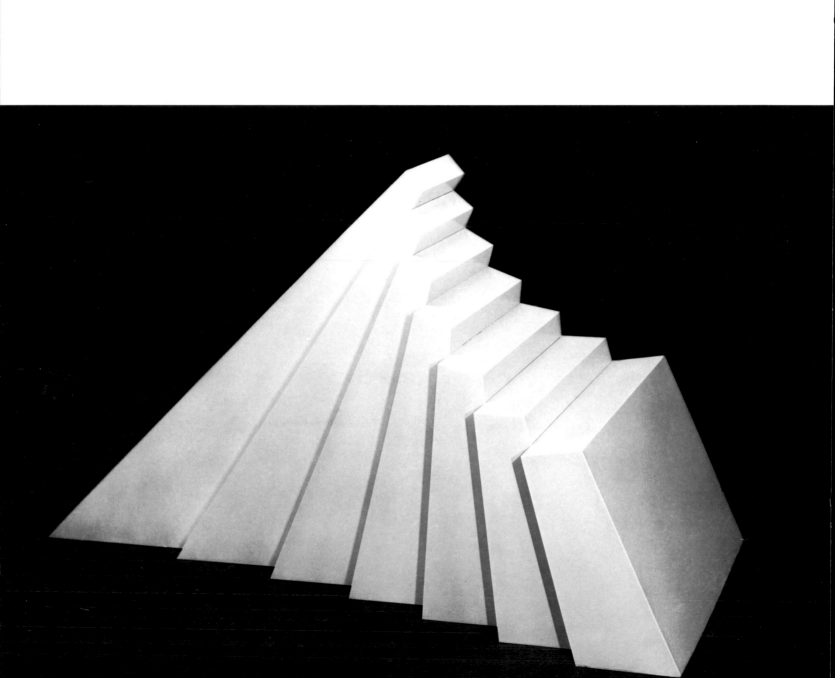

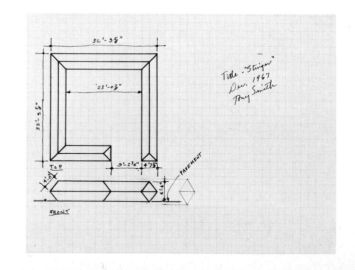

Opposite:
Robert Smithson. *Leaning Strata.* 1968. Painted steel, 3 feet x 7 feet 6 inches x 2 feet 6 inches. Dwan Gallery, New York

Above:
Tony Smith. Model for *Stinger.* 1967. Painted plywood, 6 x 32 x 32 inches

Right:
Tony Smith. Study for *Stinger.* 1967. Pen and ink on graph paper

Opposite:

John McCracken. *There's No Reason Not To.* 1967. Polyester resin, 10 feet x 20 inches x 3 inches. Nicholas Wilder Gallery, Los Angeles, and Robert Elkon Gallery, New York

Above:

Ralph Humphrey. *Alma Court.* 1958. Oil on canvas, 72 x 60 inches. Collection Betty Parsons, New York

Above:
Ellsworth Kelly. Model for untitled sculpture. 1968. Painted cardboard, 11 inches high

Opposite:
Ellsworth Kelly. Study for untitled painting. 1968. Painted papers on cardboard, 24>8 inches high x
55 inches wide

Above:
Doug Ohlson. Untitled. 1968. Acrylic on canvas, 7 feet 6 inches x 17 feet 3 inches (ten panels, each 18 inches wide, at 3-inch intervals). Fischbach Gallery, New York

Opposite:
Patricia Johanson. *William Clark*. 1967. Oil on canvas, 8 feet 6 inches x 28 feet. Tibor de Nagy Gallery, New York

Frank Stella. Study for *Gur II*. 1967. Watercolor on graph paper

Catalogue of the Exhibition
July 3-September 8, 1968

Dimensions are given in feet and inches, height preceding width and depth.

Carl Andre. Born in Quincy, Massachusetts, 1935; lives in New York.

1 *Cedar Piece.* 1960-1964. Cedarwood, 72 x 36¼ x 36¼ inches. Collection Hollis Frampton, New York. *Illus. p. 27*

2 *Fall.* 1968. Hot rolled steel, 6 x 49 x 6 feet (21 sections, each 6 feet x 28 inches x ½ inch). Dwan Gallery, New York. *Study illus. p. 46*

Darby Bannard. Born in New Haven, Connecticut, 1931; lives in Princeton, New Jersey.

3 *Allure-Allure.* 1961. Oil on canvas, 67 x 63 inches. Owned by the artist, lent courtesy Tibor de Nagy Gallery, New York. *Illus. p. 35*

Paul Feeley. Born in Des Moines, Iowa, 1910; died in New York, 1966.

4 *Ilion.* 1962. Oil on canvas, 60 x 48 inches. Estate of the artist, courtesy Betty Parsons Gallery, New York. *Illus. p. 33*

5 *Alphecca.* 1965. Oil on canvas, 60 x 60 inches. Estate of the artist, courtesy Betty Parsons Gallery, New York. *Illus. p. 31*

6 *Grafias.* 1965. Enamel on canvas, 92 x 92 inches. Collection Helen Webster Feeley, North Bennington, Vermont. *Illus. p. 32*

7 *Deneb-El-Algedi.* 1965. Painted plywood, 36 x 36 x 36 inches. Estate of the artist, courtesy Betty Parsons Gallery, New York. *Illus. p. 30*

8 *Jack II.* 1965-1968. Gold leaf on fiber glass, 91 x 91 x 91 inches. Estate of the artist, courtesy Betty Parsons Gallery, New York. *Model illus. p. 30*

Ralph Humphrey. Born in Youngstown, Ohio, 1932; lives in New York.

9 *Alma Court.* 1958. Oil on canvas, 72 x 60 inches. Collection Betty Parsons, New York. *Illus. p. 51*

Robert Huot. Born in Staten Island, New York, 1935; lives in New York.

10 *Two Suits.* 1967. Alkyd paint on canvas, 61 x 61 inches. Collection Seth Siegelaub, New York

Patricia Johanson. Born in New York, 1940; lives in New York.

11 *William Clark.* 1967. Oil on canvas, 8 feet 6 inches x 28 feet. Tibor de Nagy Gallery, New York. *Illus. p. 55*

Jasper Johns. Born in Allendale, South Carolina, 1930; lives in New York.

12 *Flag.* 1954. Encaustic on newspaper over composition board, 42⅜ x 60¾ inches. Collection Philip Johnson, New York. *Illus. p. 21*

13 *White Numbers.* 1957. Encaustic on canvas, 34 x 28⅛ inches. The Museum of Modern Art, New York, Elizabeth Bliss Parkinson Fund. *Illus. p. 20*

Donald Judd. Born in Excelsior Springs, Missouri, 1928; lives in New York.

14 Untitled. 1963. Painted wood and galvanized iron, 49⅞ x 42 x 5½ inches. Owned by the artist. *Illus. p. 42*

15 Untitled. 1965. Galvanized iron, 11 feet 3 inches high (8 boxes, each 9 x 40 x 31 inches, at 9-inch intervals). Collection Henry Geldzahler, New York. *Illus. p. 41*

Ellsworth Kelly. Born in Newburgh, New York, 1923; lives in New York.

16 *Window (Museum of Modern Art, Paris).* 1949. Oil on canvas, and wood, 50½ x 19½ inches. Owned by the artist. *Illus. p. 13*

17 *Colors for a Large Wall.* 1951. Oil on canvas, 64 joined panels, 8 x 8 feet. Sidney Janis Gallery, New York. *Illus. p. 24*

18 *Painting for a White Wall.* 1952. Oil on canvas, 5 joined panels, 23½ x 71½ inches. Owned by the artist. *Illus. p. 25*

19 *White Relief—Arch and Its Shadow (Pont de la Tournelle, Paris).* 1952-1955. Painted wood, 64 x 48 inches. Private collection, London. *Illus. p. 23*

20 Untitled. 1968. Oil on canvas, 5 joined panels, 120>40 inches high x 22 feet 7 inches wide. Sidney Janis Gallery, New York. *Study illus. p. 53*

21 Untitled. 1968. Painted steel, 9 feet 6 inches x 16 feet x 8 feet 6 inches (approx.). Sidney Janis Gallery, New York. *Model illus. p. 52*

Lyman Kipp. Born in Dobbs Ferry, New York, 1929; lives in North Salem, New York.

22 *Albatross.* 1968. Painted steel, 96 x 90 x 48 inches. Owned by the artist. *Model illus. p. 44*

Sol LeWitt. Born in Hartford, Connecticut, 1928; lives in New York.

23 Untitled. 1966-1968. Baked enamel on steel, 2 x 12 x 12 feet. Dwan Gallery, New York. *Model illus. p. 43*

Alexander Liberman. Born in Kiev, Russia, 1912; to U.S.A., 1941; lives in New York.

24 *Minimum.* 1950. Enamel on composition board, 48 x 48 inches. Owned by the artist. *Illus. p. 22*

Morris Louis. Born in Baltimore, Maryland, 1912; died in Washington, D.C., 1962.

25 *Alpha Tau.* 1961. Acrylic on canvas, 8 feet 6 inches x 19 feet 6 inches. City Art Museum of St. Louis, gift of the Shoenberg Foundation. *Illus. p. 39*

John McCracken. Born in Berkeley, California, 1934; lives in Venice, California.

26 *There's No Reason Not To.* 1967. Polyester resin, 10 feet x 20 inches x 3 inches. Nicholas Wilder Gallery, Los Angeles, and Robert Elkon Gallery, New York. *Illus. p. 50*

Agnes Martin. Born in Macklin, Saskatchewan, Canada, 1912; to U.S.A. 1932; lives in New York.

27 *Bones Number 2.* 1961. Oil on canvas, 72 x 48 inches. Collection Betty Parsons, New York. *Illus. p. 40*

Antoni Milkowski. Born in Evanston, Illinois, 1935; lives in East Chatham, New York.

28 Untitled. 1968. Stainless steel, 4 x 4 x 12 feet. Tibor de Nagy Gallery, New York.

Robert Morris. Born in Kansas City, Missouri, 1931; lives in New York.

29 *Slab.* 1962-1968. Painted steel, 8 inches x 8 feet x 8 feet. Leo Castelli Gallery, New York

30 Untitled. 1967-1968. Aluminum I-beams, 4 feet 6 inches x 15 feet x 15 feet. Leo Castelli Gallery, New York. *Illus. p. 47*

Barnett Newman. Born in New York, 1905; lives in New York.

31 *Here.* 1950. Bronze, 8 feet x 27 inches x 26 inches. Collection Mrs. Barnett Newman, New York. *Illus. p. 18*

32 *Day One.* 1951. Oil on canvas, 11 feet x 4 feet 2¼ inches. Whitney Museum of American Art, New York, gift of the Friends of the Whitney Museum and purchase. *Illus. p. 15*

33 *Ulysses.* 1952. Oil on canvas, 11 feet x 4 feet 2 inches. Collection Mrs. Barnett Newman. New York. *Illus. p. 15*

Kenneth Noland. Born in Asheville, North Carolina, 1924; lives in New York.

34 *Turnsole.* 1961. Oil on canvas, 7 feet 10⅛ inches x 7 feet 10⅛

inches. The Museum of Modern Art, New York, Blanchette Rockefeller Fund. *Illus. p. 38*

35 *Resta.* 1968. Polymer vinyl paint on canvas, 7 feet 6 inches x 29 feet. Owned by the artist

Doug Ohlson. Born in Cherokee, Iowa, 1936; lives in New York.

36 Untitled. 1968. Acrylic on canvas, 7 feet 6 inches x 17 feet 3 inches (ten panels, each 18 inches wide, at 3-inch intervals). Fischbach Gallery, New York. *Illus. p. 54*

Georgia O'Keeffe. Born in Sun Prairie, Wisconsin, 1887; lives in Abiquiu, New Mexico.

37 *Blue Lines Number 10.* 1916. Watercolor on paper, 25 x 19 inches. Lent by Georgia O'Keeffe and The Metropolitan Museum of Art, Alfred Stieglitz Collection, 1949. *Illus. p. 10*

38 *Lake George Window.* 1929. Oil on canvas, 40 x 30 inches. The Museum of Modern Art, New York, acquired through the Richard D. Brixey Bequest. *Illus. p. 12*

Raymond Parker. Born in Beresford, South Dakota, 1922; lives in New York.

39 *Number 100.* 1962. Oil on canvas, 77 x 68 inches. Owned by the artist. *Illus. p. 34*

Jackson Pollock. Born in Cody, Wyoming, 1912; died in East Hampton, New York, 1956.

40 *Number 1.* 1948. Oil on canvas, 5 feet 8 inches x 8 feet 8 inches. The Museum of Modern Art, New York, purchase. *Illus. p. 17*

Larry Poons. Born in Japan, 1937; to U.S.A., 1938; lives in New York.

41 *Knoxville.* 1966. Acrylic on canvas, 10 feet x 13 feet 3 inches. Collection Marie-Christophe Thurman, New York

Ad Reinhardt. Born in Buffalo, New York, 1913; died in New York, 1967.

42 *Ultimate Painting.* 1953-1960. Oil on canvas, 43 x 43 inches. Collection Betty Parsons, New York

Mark Rothko. Born in Dvinsk, Russia, 1903; to U.S.A., 1913; lives in New York.

43 *Number 10.* 1950. Oil on canvas, 90⅜ x 57⅛ inches. The Museum of Modern Art, New York, gift of Philip Johnson. *Illus. p. 14*

David Smith. Born in Decatur, Indiana, 1906; died in Albany, New York, 1965.

44 *Five Units Equal.* 1956. Stainless steel, 74¼ x 16¼ x 14¼ inches. Storm King Art Center, Mountainville, New York. *Illus. p. 26*

Tony Smith. Born in South Orange, New Jersey, 1912; lives in South Orange.

45 *The Louisenberg.* 1953-1954. Oil on canvas, 9 feet 9 inches x 11 feet 7 inches (11 works from a modular series):
Number 1, 24 x 32 inches. Fischbach Gallery, New York.
Number 2, 39½ x 39½ inches. Fischbach Gallery, New York.
Number 3, 39½ x 32 inches. Collection Donald Windham, New York.

Number 4, 39½ x 55 inches. Fischbach Gallery, New York.
Number 5, 20½ x 40 inches. Collection Samuel J. Wagstaff, Jr., Hartford, Connecticut.
Number 6, 39 x 23½ inches. Fischbach Gallery, New York.
Number 7, 16 x 16 inches. Fischbach Gallery, New York.
Number 8, 19¾ x 27½ inches. Fischbach Gallery, New York.
Number 9, 16 x 24 inches. Fischbach Gallery, New York.
Number 10, 8 x 15¾ inches. Fischbach Gallery, New York.
Number 11, 16 x 47½ inches. Fischbach Gallery, New York.
All illus. p. 19

46 *Free Ride.* 1962. Steel, 6 feet 8 inches x 6 feet 8 inches x 6 feet 8 inches. Collection David M. Pincus, Wynnewood, Pennsylvania. *Illus. p. 37*

47 *Die.* 1962. Steel, 6 x 6 x 6 feet. Collection Samuel J. Wagstaff, Jr., Hartford, Connecticut. *Illus. p. 36*

48 *Stinger.* 1968. Painted plywood mock-up for sculpture to be made in steel, 6 x 32 x 32 feet (approx.). Fischbach Gallery, New York. *Study and model illus. p. 49*

Robert Smithson. Born in Passaic, New Jersey, 1938; lives in New York.

49 *Leaning Strata.* 1968. Painted steel, 3 feet x 7 feet 6 inches x 2 feet 6 inches. Dwan Gallery, New York. *Illus. p. 48*

Frank Stella. Born in Malden, Massachusetts, 1936; lives in New York.

50 *Turkish Mambo.* 1959-1960. Oil on canvas, 11 feet 6 inches x 7 feet 6¾ inches. Private collection, New York. *Illus. p. 28*

51 *Six Mile Bottom.* 1960. Metallic paint on canvas, 10 x 6 feet. Collection Steve Schapiro, New York.

52 *Dade City.* 1962. Oil on canvas, 3 x 6 feet. Collection Lewis Cabot, Boston.

53 *Tuftonboro I.* 1966. Synthetic polymer paint on canvas, 8 feet 3 inches x 9 feet 1 inch. Collection Mr. and Mrs. Victor W. Ganz, New York. *Illus. p. 29*

54 *Gur II.* 1967. Synthetic polymer paint on canvas, 10 x 15 feet. Collection David Whitney, New York. *Study illus. p. 56*

Clyfford Still. Born in Grandin, North Dakota, 1904; lives in Westminster, Maryland.

55 *Painting.* 1951. Oil on canvas, 7 feet 10 inches x 6 feet 10 inches. The Museum of Modern Art, New York, Blanchette Rockefeller Fund. *Illus. p. 16*

Robert Swain. Born in Austin, Texas, 1940; lives in New York.

56 Untitled. 1967. Oil on canvas, 6 feet 8 inches x 9 feet 2 inches. Fischbach Gallery, New York.

Sanford Wurmfeld. Born in New York, 1942; lives in New York.

57 *III—12.* 1967-1968. Painted wood, 7 feet 6 inches high, diameter 30 inches. Owned by the artist, lent courtesy Tibor de Nagy Gallery, New York. *Illus. p. 45.*

Bibliography
Compiled by Bernard Karpel

This is a selective, even suggestive bibliography, especially in areas where other bibliographical material exists. Further reviews and illustrations may be located in *The Art Index,* as well as in recent biographical and bibliographical summaries to which attention is drawn below (e.g., bibls. 8, 16, 25, 28, 30). Fairly comprehensive references have been supplied for the previous writings of the author of this catalogue, and for articles and reviews about lesser-known artists whose work has received relatively little attention in print.

GENERAL REFERENCES: BOOKS

1. Battcock, Gregory, ed. *Minimal Art: A Critical Anthology.* New York: E. P. Dutton & Co., 1968.
    Includes "Two Exhibitions," by E. C. Goossen, pp. 165-174.

2. _____, ed. *The New Art: A Critical Anthology.* New York: E. P. Dutton & Co., 1966. 254 pp., illus.
    Partial contents: "The Big Canvas," by E. C. Goossen, pp. 48–56 (*see also* bibl. 39); "New Directions in American Painting," by Sam Hunter, pp. 57–66; "New York Letter 1965: Reinhardt, Duchamp, Morris," by Lucy R. Lippard, pp. 187–198; "Writings," by Ad Reinhardt, pp. 199–209; "Jasper Johns: Stories and Ideas," by John Cage, pp. 220–225.

3. Greenberg, Clement. *Art and Culture: Critical Essays.* Boston: Beacon Press, 1961. 278 pp.
    Includes "The New Sculpture," pp. 139–145; "David Smith," pp. 203–207; " 'American-Type' Painting," pp. 208–229 (*see also* bibl. 42).

4. Hess, Thomas B. *Abstract Painting: Background and American Phase.* New York: Viking Press, 1951. 164 pp., illus.

5. Hunter, Sam. "American Art Since 1945," in *New Art Around the World: Painting and Sculpture,* ed. Will Grohmann. New York: Harry N. Abrams, Inc., 1966. pp. 9–58, illus.

6. *Metro. International Directory of Contemporary Art.* Milan: Editoriale Metro, 1964. 400 pp., illus.

7. Nordness, Lee, ed. *Art: USA: Now.* New York: Viking Press, 1963. 2 vols., 475 pp., illus.
    Text by Allen S. Weller.

8. Ponente, Nello. *Contemporary Trends.* ("Modern Painting.") Lausanne: Editions d'Art Albert Skira, 1960, pp. 125–160, illus. Biographical notes, bibl.

9. Rickey, George. *Constructivism: Origins and Evolution.* New York: George Braziller, 1967. 305 pp., illus.
    Extensive bibl. by Bernard Karpel.

10. Ritchie, Andrew Carnduff. *Abstract Painting and Sculpture in America.* New York: The Museum of Modern Art, 1951. 159 pp., illus.
    Catalogue of exhibition, bibl.

11. Rose, Barbara. *American Art Since 1900: A Critical History.* [Vol. 1]. New York: Frederick A. Praeger, 1967. 320 pp., illus.
    Ch. 8: "After Abstract Expressionism," pp. 211–237; Ch. 9: "Toward a Sculptural Renaissance," pp. 238–269; bibl.

12. _____, ed. *Readings in American Art Since 1900: A Documentary Survey.* [Vol. 2]. New York: Frederick A. Praeger, 1968. 224 pp., illus., bibl.

13. Rosenberg, Harold. *The Anxious Object: Art Today and Its Audience.* New York: Horizon Press, 1964. 270 pp., illus.

GENERAL REFERENCES: EXHIBITION CATALOGUES
(arranged chronologically)

14. New York. The Museum of Modern Art, International Program. *The New American Painting as Shown in Eight European Countries 1958–1959.* 1959. 96 pp., illus.
    Introduction by Alfred H. Barr, Jr. Statements, biographies, bibl. Exhibition shown at Basel, Kunsthalle, Apr. 19–May 26, 1958; Milan, Galleria Civica d'Arte Moderna, June 1–29; Madrid, Museo Nacional de Arte Contemporáneo, July 16–Aug. 11; Berlin, Hochschule für Bildende Künste, Sept. 1–Oct. 1; Amsterdam, Stedelijk Museum, Oct. 17–Nov. 24; Brussels, Palais des Beaux-Arts, Dec. 6, 1958–Jan. 4, 1959; Paris, Musée National d'Art Moderne, Jan. 16–Feb. 15; London, Tate Gallery, Feb. 24–Mar. 23.

15. New York. The Museum of Modern Art. *Sixteen Americans.* Ed., Dorothy C. Miller. Dec. 16, 1959–Feb. 14, 1960. 96 pp., illus.
    Statements, biographies.

16. New York. The Solomon R. Guggenheim Museum. *American Abstract Expressionists and Imagists.* Oct.–Dec. 1961. 131 pp., illus.
    Introduction by H. H. Arnason, biographies, extensive bibl. by Susi Bloch.

17. New York. Whitney Museum of American Art. *Geometric Abstraction in America.* Mar. 20–May 13, 1962. 68 pp., illus.
    Text by John Gordon.

18. New York. Jewish Museum. *Toward a New Abstraction.* May 19– Sept. 15, 1963. 40 pp., illus.
    Introduction by Ben Heller. Texts by Henry Geldzahler, Robert Rosenblum, Alan R. Solomon, Ulfert Wilke, and Michael Fried. Biographies, bibl.

19. Washington, D.C. Washington Gallery of Modern Art. *Formalists.* June 6–July 7, 1963. 14 pp., illus.
    Introduction by Adelyn D. Breeskin.

20. Los Angeles County Museum of Art. *Post Painterly Abstraction.* Apr. 23–June 7, 1964. 93 pp., illus.
    Text by Clement Greenberg. Exhibition also shown at Walker Art Center, Minneapolis, July 13–Aug. 16; The Art Gallery of Ontario, Toronto, Nov. 20–Dec. 20. (*See also* bibl. 45.)

21. Yonkers, N. Y. Hudson River Museum. *8 Young Artists: Carl Andre, Walter Darby Bannard, Robert Barry, Robert Huot, Patricia Johanson, Antoni Milkowski, Douglas Ohlson, Terence Syverson.* Oct. 11–25, 1964. [24] pp., illus.
    Painting and sculpture selected by E. C. Goossen. Introduction, biographical notes.

22. New York. The Museum of Modern Art. *The Responsive Eye.* Feb. 23–Apr. 25, 1965. 56 pp., illus.
    Text by William C. Seitz. Exhibition also shown at City Art Museum of St. Louis, May 20–June 20; Seattle Art Museum, July 15– Aug. 23; Pasadena Art Museum, Sept. 28–Nov. 7; Baltimore Museum of Art, Dec. 14, 1965–Jan. 23, 1966.

23. Cambridge, Mass. Fogg Art Museum. *Three American Painters: Kenneth Noland, Jules Olitski, Frank Stella.* Apr. 21–May 30, 1965. 80 pp., illus.

Introduction by Michael Fried, chrons. Exhibition also shown at Pasadena, Cal., July 6–Aug. 3. Part I of Introduction previously published as "Modernist Painting and Formal Criticism," *The American Scholar*, Autumn 1964, pp. 642–648; Part III as text for Kenneth Noland catalogue for Jewish Museum exhibition, 1965 (bibl. 119).

24. Washington, D.C. Washington Gallery of Modern Art. *The Washington Color Painters*. June 25–Sept. 5, 1965. 50 pp., illus.
    Text by Gerald Nordland, bibl. Exhibition also shown at Austin, Tex.; Santa Barbara, Cal.; Rose Art Museum, Brandeis University, Waltham, Mass.; Walker Art Center, Minneapolis.

25. Los Angeles County Museum of Art. *New York School. The First Generation: Paintings of the 1940s and 1950s.* Ed., Maurice Tuchman. July 16–Aug. 1, 1965. 253 pp., illus.
    Statements by artists and critics, chrons., bibl. by Lucy R. Lippard.

26. São Paulo. VIII Bienal. *The United States of America.* Sept. 4–Nov. 28, 1965. [73] pp., illus.
    Organized by the Pasadena Museum. Text by Walter Hopps, biographies, bibl. Exhibition also shown at the National Collection of Fine Arts, Smithsonian Institution, Washington, D.C., Jan. 27–Mar. 6, 1966.

27. San Francisco Museum of Art. *Colorists 1950–1960.* Oct. 15–Nov. 21, 1965. [76] pp., illus.
    Introduction by Anita Ventura, biographies, bibl.

28. New York. Jewish Museum. *Primary Structures: Younger American and British Sculptors.* Apr. 27–June 12, 1966. [51] pp., illus.
    Introduction by Kynaston McShine. Statements, bibl. by Katherine Kline. A symposium on the exhibit, held May 3, with Barbara Rose, Robert Morris, Donald Judd, Mark Di Suvero, and Kynaston McShine as moderator, produced an unpublished transcript, "The New Sculpture." An enlarged bibl., in manuscript, is in the Jewish Museum and The Museum of Modern Art libraries.

29. New York. The Museum of Modern Art, International Program. *Two Decades of American Painting.* 1966–1967.
    Variant catalogues issued. Exhibition shown in Japan, India, and Australia. Essays by Irving Sandler, Lucy R. Lippard, and G. R. Swenson, in English, inserted into Japanese edition; biographical notes.

30. New York. The Solomon R. Guggenheim Museum. *Systemic Painting.* Sept.–Nov. 1966. 65 pp., illus.
    Introduction by Lawrence Alloway, bibl. Reviewed by Robert Pincus-Witten, *Artforum* (New York), Nov. 1966, pp. 42-45.

31. Minneapolis, Walker Art Center. *Eight Sculptors: The Ambiguous Image.* Oct. 22–Dec. 4, 1966. [42] pp., illus.
    Text by Martin Friedman, biographies, bibl.

32. Los Angeles County Museum of Art. *American Sculpture of the Sixties.* Ed., Maurice Tuchman. Apr. 28–June 25, 1967. 258 pp., illus.
    Includes essays by Lawrence Alloway, John Coplans, Clement Greenberg, Lucy R. Lippard, Barbara Rose, and Irving Sandler, statements, bibl. Exhibition also shown at Philadelphia Museum of Art, Sept. 15–Oct. 29.

33. Washington, D.C. Washington Gallery of Modern Art. *A New Aesthetic.* May 6–June 25, 1967. 63 pp., illus.
    Text by Barbara Rose, biographies.

34. Frankfort, Germany. Frankfurter Kunstverein. *Kompass New York.* Dec. 30, 1967–Feb. 11, 1968. 52 pp., illus.
    English and German text by J. Leering. Exhibition also shown at Abbemuseum, Eindhoven, The Netherlands, Nov. 9–Dec. 17, 1967.

35. Buffalo. Albright-Knox Art Gallery. *Plus by Minus: Today's Half Century.* Mar. 3–Apr. 14, 1968. 64 pp., illus.
    Introduction by Douglas MacAgy, biographical notes.

GENERAL REFERENCES: ARTICLES

36. "American Sculpture: Special Issue." *Artforum* (New York), Summer 1967, illus.
    Articles by Philip Leider, Michael Fried, Robert Morris, Robert Smithson, Barbara Rose, Jane Harrison Cone, Sol LeWitt.

37. Antin, David. "Differences–Sames: New York 1966–1967," *Metro* (Rome), Feb. 1968, pp. 79–104, illus.

38. Goldwater, Robert. "Reflections on the New York School," *Quadrum* (Brussels), No. 8, 1960, pp. 17–36, illus.

39. Goossen, E. C. "The Big Canvas." *Art International* (Zurich), Nov. 1958, pp. 45–47.
    Reprinted in *The New Art* (bibl. 2).

40. _____. "Distillation: A Joint Showing," *Artforum* (New York), Nov. 1966, pp. 31–33, illus.
    Review of exhibition at the Stable and Tibor de Nagy galleries.

41. Greenberg, Clement. "After Abstract Expressionism," *Art International* (Zurich), Oct. 1962, pp. 24–32, illus.
    Response by Max Kozloff, June 1963, pp. 88–92.

42. _____. " 'American-Type' Painting," *Partisan Review* (New York), Spring 1955, pp. 179–196 (*see also* bibl. 3).

43. _____. "The 'Crisis' of Abstract Art," *Arts Yearbook* (New York), No. 7, 1964, pp. 89–92.

44. _____. "Modernist Painting," *Arts Yearbook* (New York), No. 4, 1961, pp. 101–108.
    Reprinted in *Art and Literature* (Lausanne), Spring 1965, pp. 193–201.

45. _____. "Post Painterly Abstraction," *Art International* (Zurich), Summer 1964, pp. 63–65, illus.
    Originally introduction for Los Angeles County Museum exhibition catalogue (bibl. 20).

46. Kozloff, Max. "American Sculpture in Transition," *Arts Magazine* (New York), May–June 1964, pp. 19–25, illus.

47. _____. "The Further Adventures of American Sculpture," *Arts Magazine* (New York), Feb. 1965, pp. 24–31, illus.

48. Lippard, Lucy R. "Rejective Art," *Art International* (Zurich), Oct., 1966, pp. 33–37, illus.

49. _____. "The Third Stream: Constructed Paintings and Painted Structures," *Art Voices* (New York), Spring 1965, pp. 44–49, illus.

50. Michelson, Annette. "10 x 10: Concrete Reasonableness," *Artforum* (New York), Jan. 1967, pp. 30–31, illus.
    Review of exhibition at Dwan Gallery.

51. Morris, Robert. "Anti Form," *Artforum* (New York), Apr. 1968, pp. 33–35, illus.

52. _____. "Notes on Sculpture," I, II, III, *Artforum* (New York),

Feb. 1966, pp. 42–44; Oct. 1966, pp. 20-23; June 1967, pp. 24–29; all illus.

53. Perreault, John. "A Minimal Future? Union Made," *Arts Magazine* (New York), Mar. 1967, pp. 26–31.

54. Rose, Barbara. "ABC Art," *Art in America* (New York), Oct.–Nov. 1965, pp. 57–69, illus.

55. _____. "Abstract Illusionism," *Artforum* (New York), Oct. 1967, pp. 33–37, illus.

56. _____. "The Second Generation: Academy and Breakthrough," *Artforum* (New York), Sept. 1965, pp. 53–63, illus.

57. Rosenblum, Robert. "The Abstract Sublime," *Art News* (New York), Feb. 1961, pp. 38–41, 56–57, illus.

58. Rubin, William S. "Younger American Painters," *Art International* (Zurich), Jan. 1960, pp. 24–31, illus.

59. Stevens, Elizabeth. "The Washington Color Painters," *Arts Magazine* (New York), Nov. 1965, pp. 30–33, illus.

INDIVIDUAL ARTISTS: BOOKS, CATALOGUES, AND ARTICLES
Carl Andre

60. Bourdon, David. "The Razed Sites of Carl Andre," *Artforum* (New York), Oct. 1966, pp. 14–17, illus.

61. Leider, Philip. [Review of exhibition at Dwan Gallery], *Artforum* (New York), Feb. 1968, pp. 46–47, illus.

62. Lippard, Lucy R. "New York Letter," *Art International* (Zurich), Sept. 1965, pp. 58–59, 67, illus.

63. Rose Barbara. "Looking at American Sculpture," *Artforum* (New York), Feb. 1965, pp. 29–36, illus.

See also bibls. 21, 28, 32, 48

Darby Bannard

64. Bannard, Darby. "Color, Paint and Present Day Painting," *Artforum* (New York), Apr. 1966, pp. 34–37, illus., bibl.

65. _____. "Cubism, Abstract Expressionism, David Smith," *Artforum* (New York), Apr. 1968, pp. 22–32, illus.

66. Krauss, Rosalind. "Darby Bannard's New Work," *Artforum* (New York), Apr. 1966, pp. 32–33, illus.

See also bibls. 11, 20, 21, 22, 28, 54

Paul Feeley

67. Alloway, Lawrence. "Paul Feeley: Introduction and Interview," *Living Arts* (London), Apr. 1964, pp. 26–47, illus.

68. Baro, Gene. "Paul Feeley: The Art of the Definite," *Arts Magazine* (New York), Feb. 1966, pp. 19–25, illus.

69. Goossen, E. C. "Paul Feeley," *Art International* (Zurich), Dec. 1964, pp. 31–33, illus.

See also bibls. 20, 22, 27, 30

Ralph Humphrey

70. Goldin, Amy. "Ralph Humphrey," *Arts Magazine* (New York), Sept.–Oct. 1965, p. 66.
    Review of exhibition at Green Gallery.

71. Kozloff, Max. "Light as Surface: Ralph Humphrey and Dan Christensen," *Artforum* (New York), Feb. 1968, pp. 26–30, illus.

See also bibls. 16, 30

Robert Huot

72. Barnitz, Jacqueline. [Review of exhibition at Radich Gallery], *Arts Magazine* (New York), May 1966, p. 62, illus.

73. Fried, Michael. "New York Letter," *Art International* (Zurich), Summer 1964, p. 82.
    Review of exhibition at Radich Gallery.

74. Poughkeepsie, N.Y. Vassar College Art Gallery. *New Directions 1964.* May 1964.
    Text by Linda Nochlin.

See also bibls. 21, 30

Patricia Johanson

75. Tillim, Sidney. "New York" [review of exhibition at Tibor De Nagy Gallery], *Artforum* (New York), Jan. 1968. pp. 53–54, illus.
    Letter from Patricia Johanson, March 1968, p. 4; reply by Mr. Tillim, pp. 4–5.

76. [Review of exhibition at Tibor De Nagy Gallery]. *Art News* (New York), Oct. 1967. p. 13.

See also bibls. 21, 40

Jasper Johns

77. Alloway, Lawrence. *Six Painters and the Object.* New York: Solomon R. Guggenheim Foundation, 1963. 26 pp., illus.
    Notes, bibl.

78. Rosenblum, Robert. "Jasper Johns," *Art International* (Zurich), Sept. 1960, pp. 75–77, illus.

79. Steinberg, Leo. *Jasper Johns.* New York: Wittenborn & Co., 1963. 45 pp., illus.
    Revised and enlarged version of essay published in *Metro,* (Rome), No. 4–5, 1962, pp. 80–109, illus., bibl.

80. Tillim, Sidney. "Ten Years of Jasper Johns," *Arts Magazine* (New York), Apr. 1964, pp. 22–26, illus.

See also bibls. 2, 6, 9, 11, 12, 15, 16, 29, 34, 58

Donald Judd

81. Glaser, Bruce. "Questions to Stella and Judd," *Art News* (New York), Sept. 1966, pp. 55–61 illus.
    Edited by Lucy R. Lippard.

82. Judd, Donald. "Specific Objects," *Arts Yearbook* (New York), No. 8, 1965, pp. 74–82, illus.

83. Krauss, Rosalind. "Allusion and Illusion in Donald Judd," *Artforum* (New York), May 1966, pp. 24–26, illus.

84. New York. Whitney Museum of American Art. *Don Judd.* Feb. 27–Mar. 24, 1968. 40 pp., illus.
    Text by William C. Agee, notes by Don Flavin, statements, chron., bibl. Reviewed by James R. Mellow, *The New York Times,* Mar. 10, 1968, Sec. D, pp. 21, 26.

85. Rose, Barbara. "Donald Judd," *Artforum* (New York), June 1965, pp. 30–32, illus.

See also bibls. 11, 12, 26, 28, 31, 32, 33, 34, 48, 63

Ellsworth Kelly

86. Geldzahler, Henry. "Interview with Ellsworth Kelly," *Art International* (Zurich), Feb. 1964, pp. 47–48, illus.
    Also published in bibl. 92.

87. Goossen, E. C. "Ellsworth Kelly," *Derrière le Miroir* (Paris), No. 110, Oct. 1958. 16 pp., illus.
    Text in French and English. Quoted, in part, in *Sixteen Americans* (bibl. 15).

88. McConathy, Dale. "Ellsworth Kelly," *Derrière le Miroir* (Paris), No. 149, Nov. 1964. 24 pp., illus.
    Text in French and English.

89. Rose, Barbara. "The Sculpture of Ellsworth Kelly," *Artforum* (New York), June 1967, pp. 51–55, illus.

90. Rubin, William S. "Ellsworth Kelly: The Big Form," *Art News* (New York), Nov. 1963, pp. 32–35, illus.

91. Tillim, Sidney. "Profiles: Ellsworth Kelly," *Arts Yearbook* (New York), No. 3, 1959, pp. 148–151, illus.

92. Washington Gallery of Modern Art. *Paintings, Sculpture and Drawings by Ellsworth Kelly.* Dec. 11, 1963–Jan. 26, 1964. 12 pp., illus.
    Exhibition also shown, with similar catalogue, Boston Institute of Contemporary Art, Feb. 1–Mar. 8, 1964.

See also bibls. 9, 11, 15, 16, 17, 18, 19, 20, 22, 28, 29, 30, 32, 34, 58

Lyman Kipp

93. Glaser, Bruce, ed. "Where Do We Go from Here?" *Arts Yearbook* (New York), No. 8, 1965, pp. 150–155, illus.
    Transcript of station WBAI (New York) broadcast with Lyman Kipp, George Sugarman, David Weinrib.

94. Pincus-Witten, Robert. "Lyman Kipp," *Artforum* (New York), Feb. 1966, p. 57, illus.
    Review of exhibition at Betty Parsons Gallery.

95. São Paulo. VII Bienal. *The United States of America: II. Ten Sculptors.* 1963, pp. [8–9], illus.
    Organized by the Walker Art Center, Minneapolis.
    Catalogue by Martin Friedman.

96. "A Survey of Recent Sculpture," *Arts Yearbook* (New York), No. 8, 1965, pp. 30–31, illus.

97. Zimmerman, Sidney. [Review of exhibition at Betty Parsons Gallery]. *Arts Magazine* (New York), Jan. 1966, p. 62.

See also bibls. 28, 63

Sol LeWitt

98. Barnitz, Jacqueline. "In the Galleries: The Box Show," *Arts Magazine* (New York), Apr. 1965, pp. 57–58.

99. LeWitt, Sol. "Paragraphs on Conceptual Art," *Artforum* (New York), Summer 1967, pp. 79–83, illus.

100. _____. "Ziggurat," *Arts Magazine* (New York), Nov. 1966, pp. 24–25.

See also bibls. 28, 32, 36, 48

Alexander Liberman

101. Butler, Barbara. "Alexander Liberman," *Art International* (Zurich), Mar. 1962, pp. 52–53, 65, illus.

102. New York. Jewish Museum. *Alexander Liberman: Recent Sculpture.* June 29–Sept. 5, 1966. Folder, illus.
    Preface by Sam Hunter, chron.

See also bibls. 9, 17, 20, 22, 32

Morris Louis

103. Boston Museum of Fine Arts. *Morris Louis 1912–1962.* Apr. 13–May 24, 1967. 84 pp., illus.
    Text by Michael Fried, chron., bibl. Appendix II: writings by Clement Greenberg. Exhibition also shown at Los Angeles County Museum of Art, Feb. 15–Mar. 26; City Art Museum of St. Louis, June 16–Aug. 6.

104. Greenberg, Clement. "Louis and Noland," *Art International* (Zurich), May 1960, pp. 26–29, illus.

105. New York. The Solomon R. Guggenheim Museum. *Morris Louis, 1912–1962.* Sept.–Oct. 1963. 32 pp., illus.
    Notes by Lawrence Alloway, bibl. by Maurice Tuchman. Reviewed by Michael Fried, *Arts Magazine* (New York), Nov. 1963, pp. 22–27; by Robert Rosenblum, *Art International* (Zurich), Dec. 1963, pp. 24–27.

106. Robbins, Daniel. "Morris Louis at the Juncture of Two Traditions," *Quadrum* (Brussels), No. 18, 1965, pp. 41–54.

107. _____. "Morris Louis: Triumph of Color," *Art News* (New York), Oct. 1963, pp. 28–29, 57–58, illus.

See also bibls. 9, 11, 16, 18, 20, 24, 27, 29, 34, 58

John McCracken

108. Coplans, John. "Art News from Los Angeles: John McCracken," *Art News* (New York), Dec. 1965, pp. 52, 61–62, illus.

109. _____. "Five Los Angeles Sculptors at Irvine," *Artforum* (New York), Feb. 1966, pp. 33–37, illus.

See also bibls. 28, 32, 33, 48

Agnes Martin

110. Hess, Thomas B. "You Can Hang It in the Hall: Op Art in the Museum of Modern Art," *Art News* (New York), April 1965, p. 43.
    Review of *The Responsive Eye* exhibition (bibl. 22).

111. J[udd], D[onald]. [Review of exhibition at Elkon Gallery], *Arts Magazine* (New York), Jan. 1964, pp. 33–34, illus.

112. London, Arthur Tooth and Sons. *6 American Abstract Painters.* Jan. 17–Feb. 18, 1961.
    Text by Lawrence Alloway. Reviewed by Roger Coleman, *Art News and Review* (London), Jan. 28–Feb. 11, 1961, p. 3.

See also bibls. 17, 19, 22, 30

Antoni Milkowski

113. I[ves], C[olta] F[eller]. [Review of exhibition at Tibor de Nagy Gallery], *Arts Magazine* (New York), Summer 1967, p. 58.

See also bibls. 21, 40

Robert Morris

114. Antin, David. "Art & Information: 1—Grey Paint, Robert Morris," *Art News* (New York), Apr. 1966, pp. 23–24, 56–58.

115. Judd, Donald, "Black, White and Gray," *Arts Magazine* (New York), Review of exhibition at Wadsworth Atheneum.

See also bibls. 2, 11, 28, 31, 32, 34, 36, 48, 50, 51, 52, 54, 63

Barnett Newman

116. Goossen, E. C. "The Philosophic Line of Barnett Newman," *Art News* (New York), Summer 1958, pp. 30–31, 62–63, illus.

117. New York. The Solomon R. Guggenheim Museum. *Barnett Newman. The Stations of the Cross: Lema Sabachthani.* Apr.–May 1966. 40 pp., illus., bibl.

See also bibls. 3, 6, 11, 12, 14, 16, 25, 26, 29, 34

Kenneth Noland

118. Bennington College, Vt. New Gallery. *Noland.* Apr. 18–May 15, 1961. Preface by E. C. Goossen (also published in Zurich: Galerie Charles Lienhard, *Kenneth Noland.* Mar. 1962).

119. New York. Jewish Museum. *Kenneth Noland.* Feb. 4–Mar. 3, 1965. 36 pp., illus. Introduction by Michael Fried, biographical notes, bibl.

120. Rose, Barbara. "Kenneth Noland," *Art International* (Zurich), Summer 1964, pp. 58–61.

See also bibls. 6, 9, 11, 16, 17, 18, 20, 22, 23, 24, 27, 29, 30, 34, 58, 104

Georgia O'Keeffe

121. Fort Worth, Tex. Amon Carter Museum of Western Art. *Georgia O'Keeffe.* Mar. 17–May 8, 1966. 30 pp., illus. Edited by Mitchell A. Wilder.

122. Goossen, E. C. "O'Keeffe," *Vogue* (New York), Mar. 1, 1967, pp. 174–179, 221–224, illus.

123. Plagens, Peter. "A Georgia O'Keeffe Retrospective in Texas," *Artforum* (New York), May 1966, pp. 27–31, illus.

124. Willard, Charlotte. "Georgia O'Keeffe," *Art in America* (New York), Oct. 1963, pp. 89–96, illus.

See also bibls. 7, 10, 11, 12

Doug Ohlson

125. Burton, Scott. "Doug Ohlson: In the Wind," *Art News* (New York), May 1968, pp. 38–39, 67–70, illus.

126. _____. [Review of exhibition at Fischbach Gallery], *Art News* (New York), Mar. 1966, p. 18.

127. W[oldman], D[iane]. [Review of exhibition at Fischbach Gallery], *Art News* (New York), Mar. 1967, p. 16.

See also bibl. 21

Raymond Parker

128. Godden, Bill. "Raymond Parker," in *School of New York: Some Younger Artists.* Ed., B. H. Friedman. New York: Grove Press, 1959, pp. 48–53, illus.

129. Parker, Raymond. "Direct Painting," *It Is* (New York), Spring 1958, p. 20.

130. _____. "Intent Painting," *It Is* (New York), Autumn 1958, pp. 8–9.

131. Washington, D.C. Washington Gallery of Modern Art. *Ray Parker.* Apr. 23–May 21, 1966. 24 pp., illus. Exhibition also shown at San Francisco Museum of Art, Jan. 20–Mar. 5; University of New Mexico, Albuquerque, Apr. 23–May 21, 1967.

See also bibls. 6, 11, 16, 18, 20, 58

Jackson Pollock

132. O'Connor, Francis V. "The Genesis of Jackson Pollock," *Artforum* (New York), May 1967, pp. 16–23, illus.

133. _____. *Jackson Pollock.* New York: The Museum of Modern Art, 1967. 148 pp., illus. Exhibition catalogue, chron., extensive bibl.

134. Rubin, William S. "Jackson Pollock and the Modern Tradition," *Artforum* (New York), Feb. 1967, pp. 14–22; Mar., pp. 28–37; Apr., pp. 18–31; May, pp. 28–33; all illus.

See also bibls. 3, 4, 8, 10, 11, 12, 14, 16, 25, 29, 34, 57

Larry Poons

135. Coplans, John. "Larry Poons," *Artforum* (New York), June 1965, pp. 33–35, illus.

136. Johnson, E. H. "Three Young Americans: Hinman, Poons, Williams," *Oberlin College Bulletin,* Spring 1965, pp. 82–86, illus. Reprinted as "Three New, Cool, Bright Imagists," *Art News* (New York), Summer 1965, pp. 42–44, 62–64, illus.

137. Tillim, Sidney. "Larry Poons, the Dotted Line," *Arts Magazine* (New York), Feb. 1965, pp. 16–21, illus.

See also bibls. 9, 11, 19, 26, 27, 29, 30, 34

Ad Reinhardt

138. New York. Jewish Museum. *Ad Reinhardt.* Nov. 22, 1966–Jan. 15, 1967. 76 pp., illus. Texts by Sam Hunter and Lucy R. Lippard, chron., comprehensive bibl.

139. Reinhardt, Ad. *Ad Reinhardt, 1960: 25 Years of Abstract Painting.* New York: Betty Parsons Gallery, 1960. 16 pp., illus. Booklet with chronology and articles by the artist reprinted from *Art News* (New York), Dec. 1954, pp. 24–27; May 1957, pp. 37–38; Jan. 1960, pp. 32–35; all illus.

See also bibls. 2, 4, 7, 9, 10, 11, 12, 16, 17, 19, 22, 25, 29, 34

Mark Rothko

140. Goossen, E. C. "The End of the Winter in New York," *Art International* (Zurich), No. 2–3, 1958, p. 37.

141. _____. "Rothko: the Omnibus Image," *Art News* (New York), Jan. 1961, pp. 38–40, 60–61, illus.

142. London. Marlborough Fine Art Ltd. *Mark Rothko.* 1964. 34 pp., illus.
Chron., bibl.

143. Selz, Peter. *Mark Rothko.* New York: The Museum of Modern Art,
Jan. 18–Mar. 12, 1961, 44 pp., illus.
Catalogue of exhibition, chron., bibl.

See also bibls. 3, 4, 6, 8, 11, 14, 16, 25, 27, 29, 34, 57

David Smith

144. Cambridge, Mass. Fogg Art Museum. *David Smith 1906–1965:
A Retrospective Exhibition.* Sept. 28–Nov. 15, 1966. 107 pp., illus.
Reprints various statements by the artist. Handlist compiled by
Jane Harrison Cone and Margaret Paul, chron., bibl.
Exhibition also shown at Washington Gallery of Modern Art,
Washington, D.C., Jan. 7–Feb. 26, 1967.

145. Goossen, E. C. "David Smith," *Arts Magazine* (New York), March 1956,
pp. 23–27, illus.

146. New York. Marlborough-Gerson Gallery. *David Smith.* October 1964.
32 pp., illus.
Includes "The Secret Letter: An Interview with David Smith,
June 1964," by Thomas B. Hess.

See also bibls. 3, 6, 9, 10, 11, 12, 17, 19, 32

Tony Smith

147. Baro, Gene. "Tony Smith: Toward Speculation in Pure Form,"
Art International (Zurich), Summer 1967, pp. 27–30.

148. Burton, Scott. "Old Master at the New Frontier," *Art News*
(New York), Dec. 1966, pp. 52–55, 68–70, illus.
On the occasion of exhibitions at Wadsworth Atheneum,
Nov. 8–Dec. 31 and Institute of Contemporary Art,
University of Pennsylvania, Nov. 21, 1966–Jan. 6, 1967.

149. Lippard, Lucy R. "Tony Smith: 'The Ineluctable Modality of the
Visible,'" *Art International* (Zurich), Summer 1967, pp. 24–26, illus.

150. Wagstaff, Samuel, Jr. "Talking with Tony Smith," *Artforum*
(New York), Dec. 1966, pp. 14–19, illus.

See also bibls. 28, 32, 115

Robert Smithson

151. Smithson, Robert. "Entropy and the New Monuments," *Artforum*
(New York), June 1966, pp. 26–31, illus.

152. _____. "The Monuments of Passaic," *Artforum* (New York),
Dec. 1967, pp. 48–51, illus.

153. _____. "Quasi-infinities and the Wanting of Space,"
Arts Magazine (New York), Nov. 1966, pp. 28–31, illus.

154. _____. "Towards the Development of an Air Terminal Site,"
Artforum (New York), June 1967, pp. 36–40, illus.

See also bibls. 28, 32, 36, 50

Frank Stella

155. Fried, Michael. "Shape as Form: Frank Stella's New Paintings,"
Artforum (New York), Nov. 1966, pp. 18–27, illus.
Bibliographical footnotes and addenda.

156. Leider, Philip. "Frank Stella," *Artforum* (New York), June 1965,
pp. 24–26, illus.

157. Rosenblum, Robert. "Frank Stella: Five Years of Variation on an
'Irreducible' Theme," *Artforum* (New York), Mar. 1965,
pp. 21–25, illus.

See also bibls. 2, 4, 9, 11, 12, 15, 16, 17, 18, 19, 20, 22, 23, 26,
27, 29, 30, 34, 57, 58, 81

Clyfford Still

158. Buffalo. Albright-Knox Art Gallery. *Paintings by Clyfford Still.*
Nov. 5–Dec. 13, 1959. [48] pp., illus.
Includes biography, and letter by the artist.

159. _____. *Clyfford Still. Thirty-three Paintings in the
Albright-Knox Art Gallery.* 1966. 87 pp., illus.
Foreword by Katharine Kuh. Biographical notes by Ethel Moore.
Statement by the artist.

160. Goossen, E. C. "Painting as Confrontation: Clyfford Still,"
Art International (Zurich), Jan. 1960, pp. 39–43, illus.

161. Philadelphia. Institute of Contemporary Art, University of
Pennsylvania. *Clyfford Still.* Oct. 18–Nov. 29, 1963. [44] pp., illus.
Introduction by Ti-Grace Sharpless.

See also bibls. 6, 8, 11, 14, 16, 25, 34, 57